A Peoples Education Skillbook for

AP*/Honors

U.S. Government and Politics

Interpreting Political Data

Peoples Education
Your partner in student success™
www.PeoplesEducation.com

Rebecca Small

About the Author
Rebecca Small teaches AP U.S. Government & Politics, AP Comparative Government & Politics, and Political Science at Herndon High School in Herndon, Virginia. She is an AP U.S. Government & Politics consultant, and has taught week-long and one-day professional development workshops for AP teachers since 2000. A former member of the AP Government & Politics Test Development Committee, Ms. Small has served as an AP exam reader since 1998, and — more recently — as an exam question leader. She is also the author of several College Board publications, including an *AP United States Government & Politics Teacher's Guide*.

Executive Editor: Doug Falk

Production: InContext Publishing Partners

Design: Steven Genzano

Cover Design: Debee Rommel

Marketing Manager: Marcie Silver

Peoples Education is the exclusive high school distributor for college-level texts published by
W. W. Norton & Company
John Wiley & Sons

Visit PeoplesCollegePrep.com

Peoples Education®
Your partner in student success™

ISBN 978-1-4138-4886-1

299 Market Street
Saddle Brook, New Jersey 07663

Printed in the United States of America.

10 9 8 7 6 5 4 3 2 1

Table *of* Contents

To the Student

Why interpret data?

According to the College Board, students who successfully complete a course in AP U.S. Government & Politics will be able to interpret political data that is presented in tables and graphs. Your teacher may expect you to study tables and graphs and decide what the numbers, lines, or bars mean. You should be able to describe the story that a table or a graph tells. You should be able to

- write about trends and patterns that you may find in data,
- explain reasons for the trends and patterns, and
- draw conclusions from them.

These are skills that you can transfer to other courses in high school and college, and to your role as an informed citizen. The skills that you practice in this book will be valuable to you when you take the AP U.S. Government & Politics exam, which will include questions that call on you to interpret data.

It is also quite likely that you will find yourself using these skills in your career, where effective decision-making depends upon skillful interpretation of data, no matter what career area you decide to enter.

How this book will help you

Interpreting Political Data provides you with 15 exercises in U.S. Government and Politics to help you practice and enhance your skills in this area.

In each exercise you will find a brief **Background** statement that gives a context for the data you will study. In some cases, the **Background** tells you what you should already know about the topic before you study the data and attempt to answer questions.

Then, under the subhead **Interpret the Data**, each exercise presents questions for you to answer. The questions call on you to study, analyze, and interpret the meaning of data presented in tables and graphs. You will get experience working with different types of graphs, such as line graphs, bar graphs, and pie charts. Most questions are free-response in form, and will call on you to write an explanation or analysis. Some of the questions require only a short answer.

To answer the questions under **Interpret the Data**, you will need to pay close attention to the column headings in tables and the labels of axes in graphs. Numbers and lines in tables and graphs are meaningless unless you know the units and quantities that have been measured, and whether the table or graph presents raw units of measurement or—in some cases—percentages.

Following the exercises, you will find several multiple-choice questions that will give you further practice in interpreting the meaning of data.

When you have completed the exercises in this book, you will not only gain in skill as a data analyst, you will also be more informed about the government and political system in the United States.

Enjoy ***Interpreting Political Data***!

EXERCISE 1

Who Has the Power – the Federal Government or the States? Part 1

Background

In the 1980's the federal government issued a "mandate" that all state legislatures create alcohol drinking ages of 21 at the local level. The consequence for any state that did not create such state legislation was the loss of funding from the federal government for the building of highways.

The federal mandate was upheld by the US Supreme Court in *South Dakota v. Dole.* Today, all fifty states and the District of Columbia have state laws requiring a drinking age of 21.

In this exercise you will be asked to examine how driving laws vary from state to state.

Interpret the Data

Study the data in the table about driving and safety laws by state.
Answer the following questions.

1. Identify at least three ways in which states differ in their safety laws for drivers. Describe the differences that you identify.

2. How has our system of federalism impacted safety laws for drivers?

3. What limitations exist for states who would like to relax their driving laws?

Driving and Driving Safety Laws by State

State	Minimum age for driver's license	Administrative license suspension	Alcohol ignition interlock device	Mandatory belt-use law seating positions	1995 Maximum allowable speed limit	2004 Maximum allowable speed limit
Alabama	17	90 days	no	front	65	70
Alaska	16 + 6 mo.	90 days	yes	all	—	65
Arizona	16	90 days	yes	front	55	75
Arkansas	16	120 days	yes	front	65	70
California	17	4 months	yes	all	55	70
Colorado	17	3 months	yes	front	65	75
Connecticut	16 + 10 mo.	90 days	no	front	55	65
Delaware	16 + 10 mo.	3 months	yes	all	—	65
DC	18	2–90 days	yes	all	55	55
Florida	18	6 months	yes	front	65	70
Georgia	18	1 year	yes	front	55	70
Hawaii	17	3 months	yes	front	—	60
Idaho	16	90 days	yes	all	65	75
Illinois	17	3 months	yes	front	65	65
Indiana	18	180 days	yes	front	65	70
Iowa	17	180 days	yes	front	55	70
Kansas	16	30 days	yes	front	65	70
Kentucky	17	—	yes	all	65	65
Louisiana	17	90 days	yes	front	65	70
Maine	16 + 6 mo.	90 days	yes	all	65	65
Maryland	17 + 9 mo.	45 days	yes	front	55	65
Massachusetts	18	90 days	yes	all	55	65
Michigan	17	—	yes	front	55	70
Minnesota	16	90 days	yes	front	65	70
Mississippi	16	90 days	yes	front	65	70
Missouri	17 + 11 mo.	30 days	yes	front	70	70
Montana	16	—	yes	all	65	75
Nebraska	17	90 days	yes	front	65	75
Nevada	18	90 days	yes	all	55	75

State	Minimum age for driver's license	Administrative license suspension	Alcohol ignition interlock device	Mandatory belt-use law seating positions	1995 Maximum allowable speed limit	2004 Maximum allowable speed limit
New Hampshire	17 + 1 mo.	6 months	yes	—	65	65
New Jersey	18	—	yes	front	—	65
New Mexico	16 + 6 mo.	90 days	yes	all	65	75
New York	17	variable	yes	all	55	65
North Carolina	16 + 6 mo.	30 days	yes	front	55	70
North Dakota	16	91 days	yes	front	65	75
Ohio	17	90 days	yes	front	65	65
Oklahoma	16 + 6 mo.	180 days	yes	front	65	75
Oregon	17	90 days	yes	all	65	65
Pennsylvania	17	—	yes	front	55	65
Rhode Island	17 + 6 mo.	—	yes	all	55	65
South Carolina	16 + 6 mo.	—	yes	all	65	70
South Dakota	16	—	no	front	65	75
Tennessee	17	—	yes	front	65	70
Texas	16 + 6 mo.	90 days	yes	front	65	75
Utah	17	90 days	yes	all	55	75
Vermont	16 + 6 mo.	90 days	no	all	65	65
Virginia	18	7 days	yes	front	65	65
Wash	17	90 days	yes	all	55	70
West Virginia	17	6 months	yes	front	65	70
Wisconsin	16 + 9 mo.	6 months	yes	front	65	65
Wyoming	16 + 6 mo.	90 days	no	all	65	75

EXERCISE 2

Who Has the Power – the Federal Government or the States? Part 2

Background

The federal minimum wage provisions are contained in the law called the Fair Labor Standards Act (FLSA). The federal minimum wage is $6.55 per hour effective July 24, 2008. During his administration, President George Bush signed a law that increases the federal minimum wage to $7.25 in July 2009. Many states also have minimum wage laws.

Interpret the Data

Study the data in the Minimum Wage table. Then, answer the following questions.

1. How many states have the same minimum wage as the wage that is required by the federal government?
2. How many states exceed the federal minimum wage?
3. How many states have either no minimum wage law, or have minimum wages lower than the federal minimum?
4. For the states you identified above in question 3, what would the minimum wage be and why?
5. Why might a state legislature wish to adopt a higher minimum wage than the federal government?
6. Why might a state legislature wish to adopt a lower minimum wage or no minimum wage?
7. Why do you suppose that so many states have higher minimum wages than the federal government?
8. Why might Congress consider legislation to raise the minimum wage? Why has the U.S. Congress enacted legislation to raise the minimum wage in 2009?

Minimum Wage Table

State	Minimum Wage – July 2008	Increased Minimum Wage	Effective Date of Increase
United States	$6.55	$7.25	24–Jul–2009
Alabama	No State Law		
Alaska	$7.15		
Arizona	$6.90		
Arkansas	$6.25		
California	$8.00		
Colorado	$7.00		
Connecticut	$7.65	$8.25	1–Jan–2010
Delaware	$7.15	$7.25	20–Jul–2009
DC	$7.55		
Florida	$6.79		
Georgia	$5.15		
Hawaii	$7.25		
Idaho	$6.55	$7.25	24–Jul–2009
Illinois	$7.75	$8.00	1–Jul–2009
Indiana	$6.55	$7.25	24–Jul–2009
Iowa	$7.25		
Kansas	$2.65		
Kentucky	$6.55	$7.25	1–Jul–2009
Louisiana	No State Law		
Maine	$7.25	$7.50	1–Oct–2009
Maryland	$6.55	$7.25	24–Jul–2009
Mass	$8.00		
Michigan	$7.40		
Minnesota	$6.15 / $5.25		
Mississippi	No State Law		
Missouri	$6.65		
Montana	$6.55	$7.25	24–Jul–2009
Nebraska	$6.55	$7.25	24–Jul–2009
Nevada	$6.85		
New Hampshire	$7.25		

State	Minimum Wage – July 2008	Increased Minimum Wage	Effective Date of Increase
New Jersey	$7.15	$7.25	24–Jul–2009
New Mexico	$7.50		
New York	$7.15	$7.25	24–Jul–2009
North Carolina	$6.55	$7.25	24–Jul–2009
North Dakota	$6.55	$7.25	24–Jul–2009
Ohio	$7.00		
Oklahoma	$6.55	$7.25	24–Jul–2009
Oregon	$7.95		
Pennsylvania	$7.15	$7.25	1–Jul–2009
Rhode Island	$7.40		
South Carolina	No State Law		
South Dakota	$6.55	$7.25	24–Jul–2009
Tennessee	No State Law		
Texas	$6.55	$7.25	24–Jul–2009
Utah	$6.55	$7.25	24–Jul–2009
Vermont	$7.68		
Virginia	$6.55	$7.25	24–Jul–2009
Washington	$8.00		
West Virginia	$7.25		
Wisconsin	$6.50		
Wyoming	$5.15		

Exercise 3

Political Culture: Trust in Federal Government

Background

The attitudes of American citizens toward the institutions of their government change over time. Major events affect the trust and confidence that people place in their government. Surveys and polls reveal how citizens' trust can shift over a period of several decades.

Interpret the Data

Study the graph entitled Trust in Federal Government, 1964–2004. The data shown in the graph are based on the following question:

How much of the time do you think you can trust the government in Washington to do what is right—just about always, most of the time, some of the time, or none of the time?

Answer the following questions.

1. What overall trend in trust in government from 1964 to 2004 is displayed in the graph?

2. Identify two major events during the years shown in the graph that may have caused the trend you described above to occur. Explain why.

3. What impact might the trend in the graph have on citizen participation?

4. What events may have caused temporary reversals of the overall trend?

Trust in Federal Government, 1964–2004

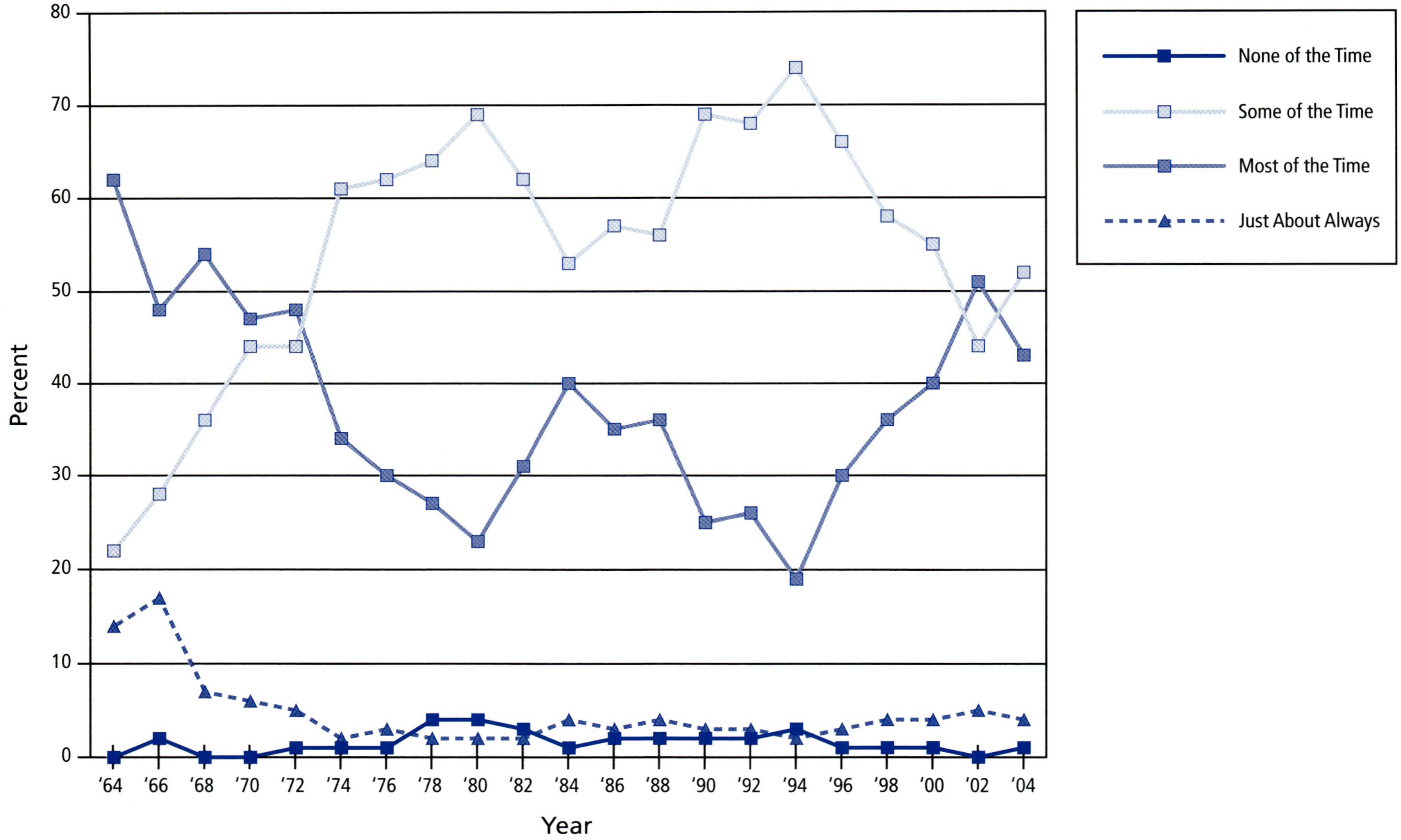

EXERCISE 4

Political Culture: Attitude Toward U.S. Congress

Background

The graph is based on survey data compiled over a 24-year period. The number of people participating in the surveys ranged from 1,200 to 2,200.

Interpret the Data

Study the graph entitled Approval of U.S. Congress, 1980–2004. The graph is based on the following question:

Do you approve or disapprove of the way the U.S. Congress has been handling its job?

Answer the following questions.

1. What is the overall trend in public attitudes toward Congress?

2. How have the attitudes changed during the years shown?

3. What might explain the changes in attitudes shown?

4. What do you find when you compare 1980 to 2004?

5. How do the two years 1980 and 2004 differ? How are they similar?

6. When did a large shift in public attitudes occur? What might explain the attitude shift that you identify?

Approval of U.S. Congress, 1980–2004

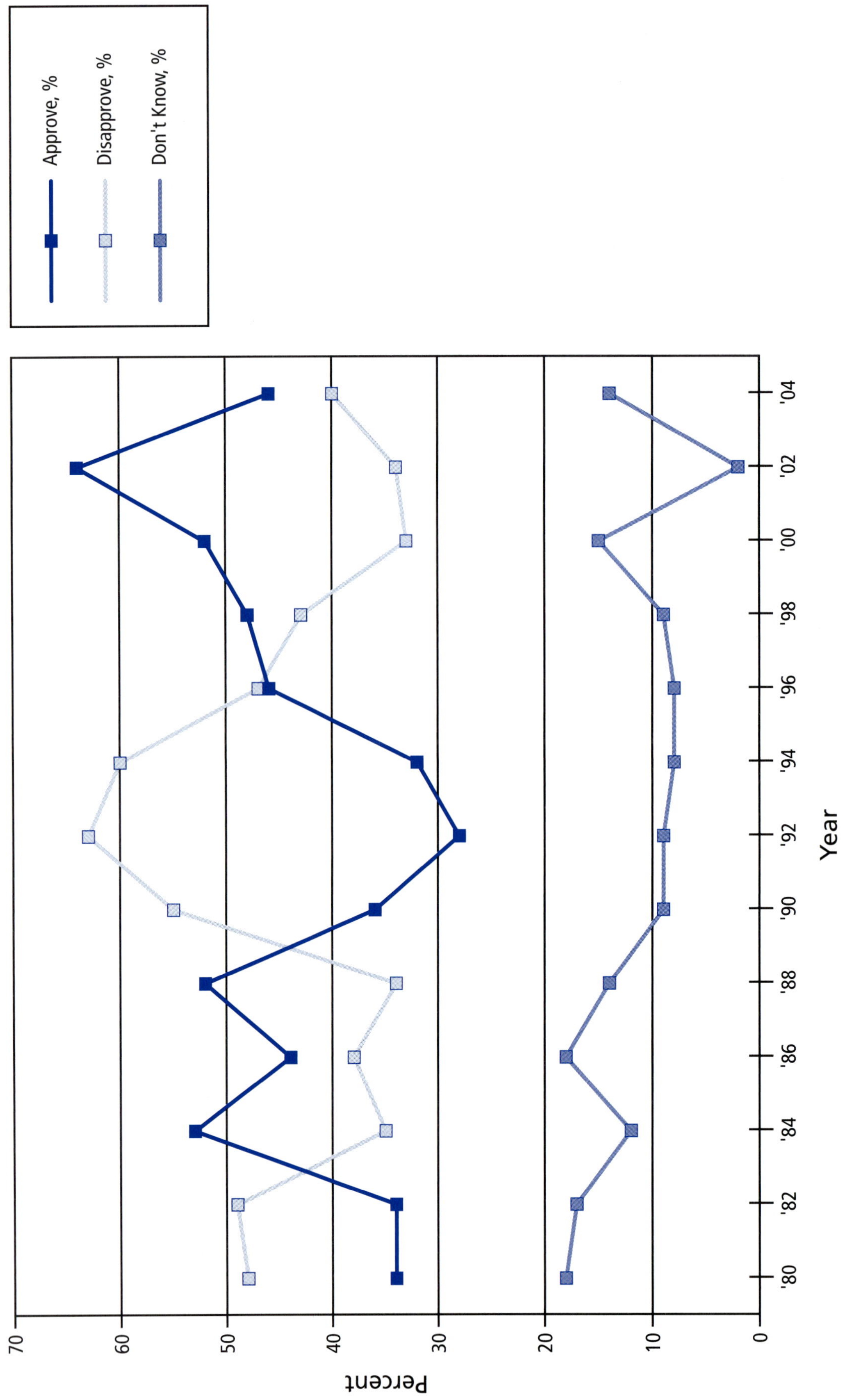

Exercise 5

Political Culture: Party Identification

Background

The information in the table was compiled from a survey question that asked:

In politics, as of today, do you consider yourself a Republican, a Democrat, or an Independent?

During the period 1952–2004, an average of 1,816 individuals per year responded to the survey question.

Interpret the Data

Study the table Party Identification, 1952–2004. Work with another student to examine and discuss the data. Answer the following questions.

1. What is the trend in the number of citizens identifying themselves as Democrats?
2. What factors explain the trend you identified in question 1?
3. What is the trend in the number of citizens identifying themselves as Republicans?
4. What factors explain the trend you identified in question 3?
5. What is the trend in the number of citizens identifying themselves as independents (not affiliating with a major organized political party)?
6. What factors explain the trend you identified in question 5?
7. What is the impact of the three trends you have identified on campaigns for the Presidency?

Party Identification, 1952–2004

Year	Democrat, %	Independent, %	Republican, %	Apolitical, %
1952	57	6	34	3
1954	56	7	33	4
1956	50	9	37	4
1958	56	7	33	4
1960	52	10	36	2
1962	54	8	35	4
1964	61	8	30	1
1966	55	12	32	1
1968	55	11	33	1
1970	54	13	32	1
1972	52	13	34	1
1974	52	15	31	3
1976	52	15	33	1
1978	54	14	30	3
1980	52	13	33	2
1982	55	11	32	2
1984	48	11	39	2
1986	51	12	36	2
1988	47	11	41	2
1990	52	10	36	2
1992	50	12	38	1
1994	47	11	41	1
1996	52	9	38	1
1998	51	11	37	2
2000	50	12	37	1
2002	49	8	43	0
2004	49	10	41	0

Exercise 6

Political Processes: Political Action Committees (PACs)

Background

Answer the following questions in your notebook.

What is a Political Action Committee (PAC)?

What was the goal of the Federal Election Campaign Act of 1974?

What were the rules of the Federal Election Campaign Act of 1974?

What did critics of the Federal Election Campaign Act allege?

What is the Federal Election Commission?

What was the Bipartisan Campaign Reform Act of 2002, also called the McCain Feingold Act?

How much money is a PAC currently entitled to give in one election cycle?

Interpret the Data

Study the table and bar graph Number of Political Action Commitees, 1974–2008. Answer the following questions.

1. What is the overall trend in the number of PACs since 1974? Describe the changes that you see in the number of PACs.

2. How might regulations in the Federal Election Campaign Act have impacted the trend you identified above in Political Action Committees and why?

3. What changes do you see in the number of PACs during the period from 1998–2008? What might be the reason or reasons for this?

Number of Political Action Committees, 1974–2008 (Even-Numbered Years)

Year	Total PACs
1974	608
1976	1,146
1978	1,653
1980	2,279
1982	3,149
1984	3,803
1986	4,092
1988	4,196
1990	4,193
1992	4,125
1994	3,933
1996	4,033
1998	3,762
2000	3,706
2002	3,865
2004	4,040
2006	4,217
2008	4,234

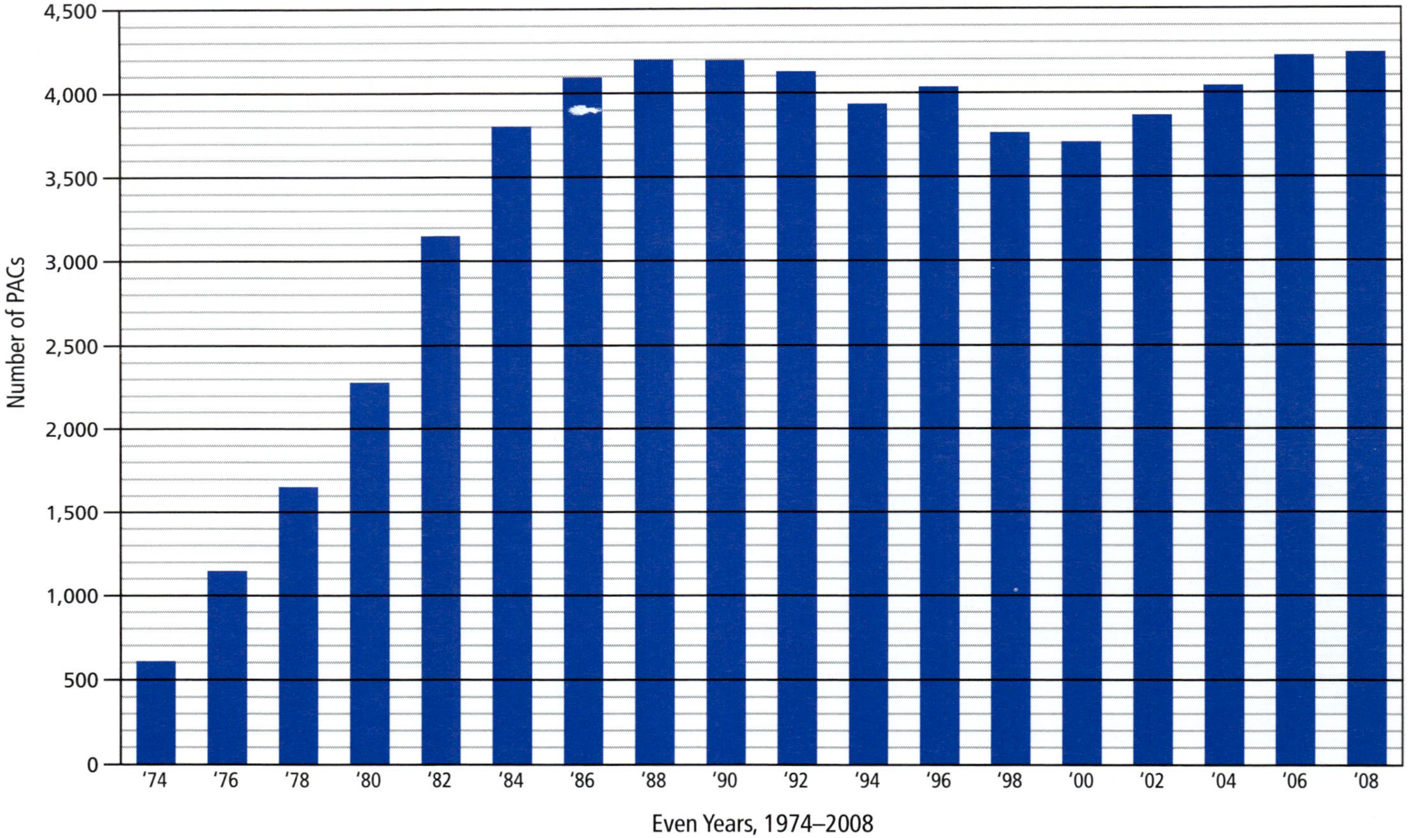

EXERCISE 7

Political Processes: Election Laws and Systems

Background

Define the following key terms. For each of the key terms, give an example of when it is used in the United States political system. Identify an advantage and a disadvantage of each.

1. plurality
2. majority
3. winner take all
4. proportional representation

Interpret the Data

Four political election scenarios are presented below. Study the table Election Systems: Determining the Outcome on the following page. Use the table to answer the questions that follow each political scenario.

1. In an election for U.S. Congress in the state of Virginia there are three candidates running for office: John Smith, a Democrat; Jane Doe, a Republican; and Larry Brown, a Libertarian. Assume 100,000 people turn out to vote.

    a) What is approximately the minimum number of votes needed to win?

    b) Why might it be difficult for the winner of the election above to claim a mandate to govern?

2. In a primary contest for delegate votes in the state of Michigan to the Republican Convention, there are three candidates: Jane Smith, David Brown, and Thomas Jackson. This year the national party is allowing Michigan to send 50 votes to the national convention. Jane Smith wins 48% of the popular vote, David Brown wins 47%, and Thomas Jackson gets 5%.

    a) How many votes to the national convention from Michigan will Jane Smith get?

    b) How many will David Brown get?

    c) How many will Thomas Jackson get?

3. In a primary election for the Democratic nomination in the state of Virginia, there are three candidates: Sally Rae, Christopher Cohn, and John Green. Assume Virginia has 20 votes to the national convention. Sally Rae wins the election with 75% of the popular vote, Christopher Cohn has 15% of the popular vote, and John Green gets 10%.

a) How many votes to the national Democratic convention will Sally Rae get?

b) How many votes to the Democratic convention will Christopher Cohn get?

c) How many votes will John Green get?

d) As an underdog, which system, Democrats or Republicans, would you favor? Why?

4. Now there is a race between Linda Thomson and Fred Ivey for the Presidency. There are a total of 538 electoral votes.

a) How many does Linda Thomson or Fred Ivey need to win?

b) Assume that Jeff Smith runs as a third party candidate in the election and wins 20% of the popular vote but no electoral votes. How would this be possible?

c) How would this change the election?

d) Assume that Jeff Smith runs and gets 34 electoral votes. How many electoral votes would Ms. Thomson now need to win?

e) Assume that Linda Thomson gets 34 electoral votes, Fred Ivey gets 220 votes, and Jeff Smith gets 18 votes. Who won the Presidency?

f) What would happen next in the above election?

Election Systems: Determining the Outcome

Type of Election	Plurality	Majority	Winner Take All	Proportional Representation
State Electoral Vote Contest	X		X	
National Presidential Election — Electoral College Votes		X		
Democratic National Convention, Contest for Delegates				X
Republican National Convention, Contest for Delegates			X	
State of Louisiana, Contest for Senate		X		
State of Virginia, Contest for House of Representatives	X			

Exercise 8

Political Processes: Voter Turnout in the United States

Background

Define the following key terms. For each of the key terms, give an example of when it is used in the United States political system.

- Voter turnout
- Suffrage
- Expansion of suffrage (for example: 19th Amendment, 15th Amendment, 26th Amendment, Civil Rights Act of 1964)
- Presidential election
- Mid-term election
- Voter registration

Interpret the Data

Study the table entitled Voter Turnout Rate in National Elections. Use information in the table and your knowledge of U.S. Government & Politics to answer the following questions.

1. What is the overall trend in voter turnout since the mid-1960s in Presidential elections?

2. List three reasons to explain this trend.

3. How does overall voter turnout in Presidential elections compare to overall voter turnout in mid-term elections?

4. List three reasons to explain this trend.

Voter Turnout Rate in National Elections

Presidential Election Year	Percent Turnout	Non-Presidential Election Year	Percent Turnout
1948	52	1950	44
1952	62	1954	44
1956	60	1958	45
1960	64	1962	48
1964	63	1966	49
1968	63	1970	47
1972	56	1974	39
1976	55	1978	39
1980	54	1982	42
1984	55	1986	38
1988	53	1990	38
1992	58	1994	41
1996	52	1998	38
2000	54	2002	40
2004	60	2006	40

EXERCISE 9

Political Processes: Voting Age Population – Registration and Voting

Background

With a partner or group, discuss the following terms. For each term, give an example of how it is used in the United States political system. Make sure that you understand how to use these terms when you discuss the political process.

- Voting-age population
- Voter-eligible population
- Voter registration

Interpret the Data

Study the table entitled Voting-Age Population: Percent Who Registered / Percent Who Voted. Use information in the table and your knowledge of U.S. Government & Politics to answer the following questions.

1. How does the "percentage who registered" compare to the "percentage who voted"?

2. Which age group or groups voted at the lowest rates in the 2000 presidential election?

3. What are the reasons for this low rate of voting?

4. How does the voting rate of whites compare to the voting rates of African Americans and Hispanics in the 2000 presidential election?

5. What is the reason for this trend?

Voting-Age Population: Percent Who Registered / Percent Who Voted
Presidential Election Years

Voting-Age Population		1988		1992		1996		2000		2004	
		% who registered	% who voted	% who registered	% who voted	% who registered	% who voted	% who registered	% who voted	% who registered	% who voted
All		67	57	68	61	66	54	64	55	66	58
Age	18–20	45	33	48	38	46	31	41	28	51	41
	21–24	51	38	55	46	51	33	49	35	52	42
	25–34	58	48	61	53	57	43	55	44	56	47
	35–44	69	61	69	64	67	55	64	55	64	57
	45–64	76	68	75	70	74	64	71	64	73	67
	65 +	78	69	78	70	77	67	76	68	77	69
Ethnicity	White	68	59	70	64	68	56	66	56	68	60
	African American	65	52	64	54	64	51	64	54	64	56
	Hispanic	57	46	59	48	59	44	57	45	58	47

Exercise 10

Political Processes: Election Realignment

Background

In 1994, a mid-term election took place during the administration of President Clinton. The Democrats had been the majority party in Congress for forty years prior to 1994. Clinton, a Democrat, had worked with a Democratic-controlled Congress for the first two years of his Presidency, but at the conclusion of the 1994 mid-term election there was a divided government.

Some political scientists wondered whether 1994 was a realigning election. In this exercise you will be asked to examine data to come up with your own answers to the following questions:

What evidence suggests that 1994 (start of the 104th Congress) was a realigning election?

What evidence suggests the contrary?

Interpret the Data

Study the following tables in order to answer the questions below.

Table 1. Impact of 1994 General Election: House and Senate.
Table 2. House of Representatives: Comparison of 103rd to 104th Congress
Table 3. Senate: Comparison of Democratic and Republican numbers, 104th Congress
Table 4. Party Membership in the House and Senate

1. How many seats in the House of Representatives did the Republican Party (GOP) gain in 1994?
2. After the 1994 mid-term election, how many state delegations had a Republican majority in the House? How many state delegations had a Democratic majority in the House?
3. In how many states did the Republicans gain House seats? In which of these states did a Democratic majority before the election become a Republican majority after the election?
4. How many states had 2 Republican Senators after the 1994 elections?
   How many states had 2 Democratic Senators after the 1994 elections?
   How many states had one Democratic and one Republican Senator after the 1994 elections?
   How many states elected a Republican Senator in the 1994 election?
5. Do you find a pattern in the outcomes of mid-term elections for the sitting President's political party? If so, describe what you find.
6. What do you think may cause this pattern to occur?

Study Table 5, 1994 State Elections for Governor.

7. How many governors were Republican after the 1994 election? How many governors were Democratic?

8. What pattern do you find in the 1994 elections for governor? Is this pattern related to the mid-term Congressional election?

Draw a conclusion by answering the next three items.

9. Describe the evidence that suggests that the 1994 election was a realignment.

10. Describe evidence that suggests that the 1994 election was not a realignment.

11. Draw a conclusion based upon your answers to questions 9 and 10. Which argument is easier to support and why?

Table 1 — Impact of 1994 General Election: House and Senate

		House of Representatives				U.S. Senate			
Years	Congress	Members	Democrats	Republicans	Other	Members	Democrats	Republicans	Other
1993–1994	103rd	435	258	176	Independent (1)	100	56	44	0
1995–1996	104th	435	204	230	Independent (1)	100	48	52	0

Table 2 — House of Representatives: Comparison of 103rd to 104th Congress

States	Democrats 103rd Congress	Democrats 104th Congress	Republicans 103rd Congress	Republicans 104th Congress	Net Change
Alabama	4	4	3	3	0
Alaska	0	1	0	1	0
Arizona	3	1	3	5	R + 2
Arkansas	2	2	2	2	0
California	30	27	22	25	R + 3
Colorado	2	2	4	4	0
Connecticut	3	3	3	3	0
Delaware	0	1	0	1	0
Florida	10	8	13	15	R + 2
Georgia	7	4	4	7	R + 3
Hawaii	2	2	0	0	0
Idaho	1	0	1	2	R + 1
Illinois	12	10	8	10	R + 2
Indiana	7	4	3	6	R + 3
Iowa	1	0	4	5	R + 1
Kansas	2	0	2	4	R + 2
Kentucky	3	2	3	4	R +1
Louisiana	4	4	3	3	0
Maine	1	1	1	1	0
Maryland	4	4	4	4	0
Massachusetts	8	8	2	2	0
Michigan	10	9	6	7	R + 1
Minnesota	6	6	2	2	0
Mississippi	5	4	0	1	R + 1
Missouri	6	6	3	3	0
Montana	1	1	0	0	0
Nebraska	1	0	2	3	R + 1
Nevada	1	0	1	2	R + 1
New Hampshire	1	0	1	2	R + 1
New Jersey	7	5	6	8	R + 2

States	Democrats		Republicans		Net Change
	103rd Congress	104th Congress	103rd Congress	104th Congress	
New Mexico	1	1	2	2	0
New York	18	17	13	14	R + 1
North Carolina	8	4	4	8	R + 4
North Dakota	1	1	0	0	0
Ohio	10	6	9	13	R + 4
Oklahoma	3	1	3	5	R + 2
Oregon	4	3	1	2	R + 1
Pennsylvania	11	11	10	10	0
Rhode Island	1	2	1	0	D + 1
South Carolina	3	2	3	4	R + 1
South Dakota	1	1	0	0	0
Tennessee	6	4	3	5	R + 2
Texas	21	19	9	11	R + 2
Utah	2	1	1	2	R + 1
Vermont	0	0	1	1	0
Virginia	7	6	4	5	R + 1
Washington	8	2	1	7	R + 6
West Virginia	3	3	0	0	0
Wisconsin	4	3	5	6	R + 1
Wyoming	0	0	1	1	0

0 = no net change
R = Republican
D = Democrat

Table 3 — Senate: Comparison of Democratic and Republican Numbers, 104th Congress

States	U.S. Senate Democrats 104th Congress	Republicans 104th Congress	Republicans Elected 1994
Alabama	1	1	
Alaska	0	2	
Arizona	0	2	
Arkansas	2	0	
California	2	0	
Colorado	1	1	
Connecticut	2	0	
Delaware	1	1	x
Florida	1	1	x
Georgia	1	1	
Hawaii	2	0	
Idaho	0	2	
Illinois	2	0	
Indiana	0	2	x
Iowa	1	1	
Kansas	0	2	
Kentucky	1	1	
Louisiana	2	0	
Maine	0	2	
Maryland	2	0	
Massachusetts	2	0	
Michigan	1	1	x
Minnesota	1	1	x
Mississippi	0	2	x
Missouri	0	2	x
Montana	1	1	x
Nebraska	2	0	
Nevada	2	0	
New Hampshire	0	2	

U.S. Senate			
States	Democrats 104th Congress	Republicans 104th Congress	Republicans Elected 1994
New Jersey	1	1	
New Mexico	1	1	
New York	1	1	
North Carolina	0	2	
North Dakota	2	0	
Ohio	1	1	x
Oklahoma	0	2	x
Oregon	0	2	
Pennsylvania	0	2	x
Rhode Island	1	1	x
South Carolina	1	1	
South Dakota	1	1	
Tennessee	0	2	x
Texas	0	2	x
Utah	0	2	x
Vermont	1	1	x
Virginia	1	1	
Washington	1	1	x
West Virginia	2	0	
Wisconsin	2	0	
Wyoming	0	2	x

x = State elected a Republican senator

Table 4 — Party Membership in the House and Senate

Party Membership		1993–1994 103rd Congress	1995–1996 104th Congress	1997–1998 105th Congress	1999–2000 106th Congress	2001–2002 107th Congress	2003–2004 108th Congress	2005–2006 109th Congress	2007–2008 110th Congress
U.S. House of Representatives 435 members	Democrats	258	204	206	211	212	204	202	233
	Republicans	176	230	228	223	221	229	232	202
	Independents	1	1	1	1	2	1	1	0
U.S. Senate 100 members	Democrats	57	48	45	45	50	48	44	49
	Republicans	43	52	55	55	49	51	55	49
	Independents	0	0	0	0	1	1	1	2

Table 5 — 1994 State Elections for Governor

State	Party of Governor before 1994 Election	Party of Governor after 1994 Election
Alabama	D	D
Alaska	D	D
Arizona	R	R
Arkansas	D	D
California	R	R
Colorado	D	D
Connecticut	I	R
Delaware	D	D
Florida	D	D
Georgia	D	D
Hawaii	D	D
Idaho	D	R
Illinois	R	R
Indiana	D	D
Iowa	R	R
Kansas	D	R
Kentucky	D	D
Louisiana	D	D
Maine	R	R
Maryland	D	D
Massachusetts	R	R
Michigan	R	R
Minnesota	R	R
Mississippi	R	R
Missouri	D	D
Montana	R	R
Nebraska	D	D
Nevada	D	D
New Hampshire	R	R
New Jersey	D	R
New Mexico	D	R
New York	D	R

State	Party of Governor before 1994 Election	Party of Governor after 1994 Election
North Carolina	D	D
North Dakota	R	R
Ohio	R	R
Oklahoma	D	R
Oregon	D	D
Pennsylvania	D	R
Rhode Island	D	R
South Carolina	R	R
South Dakota	R	R
Tennessee	D	R
Texas	D	R
Utah	R	R
Vermont	D	D
Virginia	D	R
Washington	D	D
West Virginia	D	D
Wisconsin	R	R
Wyoming	D	R

Exercise 11

Institutions of Government: Demographics of the U.S. Congress

Background

You should be familiar with the kinds of population and demographic data gathered by the U.S. Bureau of the Census. Demographic data in the census includes age, gender, race, and Hispanic origin.

Interpret the Data

Study Table 1 and Table 2. Then answer the following questions. You may use a calculator to answer some of the questions.

Part A. U.S. House of Representatives

1. Which party held a House majority in each of the following?

a) 107th Congress

b) 108th Congress

c) 109th Congress

d) 110th Congress

2. How many women are in the House of Representatives?
What percentage of the House members are women?
How does this percentage compare to the overall U.S. population?

3. How many African Americans are in the House of Representatives?
What percentage of the House is African American?
How does this percentage compare to the overall U.S. population?

4. How many Hispanic members are in the House of Representatives?
What percentage of the House is Hispanic?
How does this compare to the overall U.S. population?

Part B. U.S. Senate

5. Which party held a Senate majority in each of the following?

a) 107th Congress

b) 108th Congress

c) 109th Congress

d) 110th Congress

6. How many women are in the Senate?
What percentage of the Senate members are women?
How does this percentage compare to the overall U.S. population?

7. How many African Americans are in the Senate?
What percentage of the Senate is African American?
How does this percentage compare to the overall U.S. population?

8. How many Hispanic members are in the Senate?
What percentage of the Senate is Hispanic?
How does this compare to the overall U.S. population?

Use your responses to questions 1–8 to answer the following:

9. What conclusions can you draw about minority representation in the U.S. Congress?

10. What is the difference between minority representation in the House and minority representation in the Senate?

11. How has the number of women elected to the House and Senate changed over the years? What factors led to this trend?

12. How has the number of African Americans elected to the House and Senate changed over the years? What factors led to this trend?

13. The 110th Congressional election was a mid-term election (2006), and the President was a Republican. What happened to the Republican party in Congress?

14. The election results you described in #13 are common for mid-term elections. What factors might cause this?

Table 1 — Recent Demographics in the United States Congress

		Demographic	107th Congress	108th Congress	109th Congress	110th Congress
U.S. House of Representatives **435 Total Members**	Party Membership	Democrats	212	204	202	233
		Republicans	221	229	232	202
		Independents	2	1	1	0
	Diversity	Women	62	63	71	79
		African American	39	39	42	41
		Hispanic	19	23	24	23
U.S. Senate **100 Total Members**	Party Membership	Democrats	50	48	44	49
		Republicans	49	51	55	49
		Independents	1	1	1	2
	Diversity	Women	14	14	14	16
		African American	0	0	1	1
		Hispanic	0	0	2	3

Table 2 — Characteristics of the General U.S. Population

U.S. Census Group		Total Number	Percentage
Total		298,757,310	
Males		147,129,583	49%
Females		151,627,727	51%
Ethnic Diversity	White	221,457,175	74%
	African American	36,969,063	12%
	Asian	12,951,215	4%
	Native American	2,374,222	1%
	Other race	18,439,873	6%
	2 or more races	6,133,326	2%
	Hispanic or Latino of any race	44,019,880	15%

From the U.S. Census Bureau 2005–2007 American Community Survey

EXERCISE 12

Institutions of Government: Congressional Incumbency & Reelection

Background

Not all incumbent members of the House and Senate seek reelection. Some incumbents retire. Some are defeated in primary elections. While members of the House have 2-year terms, Senators have 6-year terms. Senate terms are staggered so that only a portion of the Senate seats are up for reelection in any one election year. For all these reasons, the number of incumbents seeking reelection is less than the number of members in each house of Congress.

Interpret the Data

Study the graph Reelection of Congressional Incumbents, then answer the following questions.

1. Identify two trends displayed in the graph.

2. Provide explanations for each of the trends you identified.

3. What consequence might these trends have?

4. What is a possible outcome or solution in response to the trend?

Reelection of Congressional Incumbents

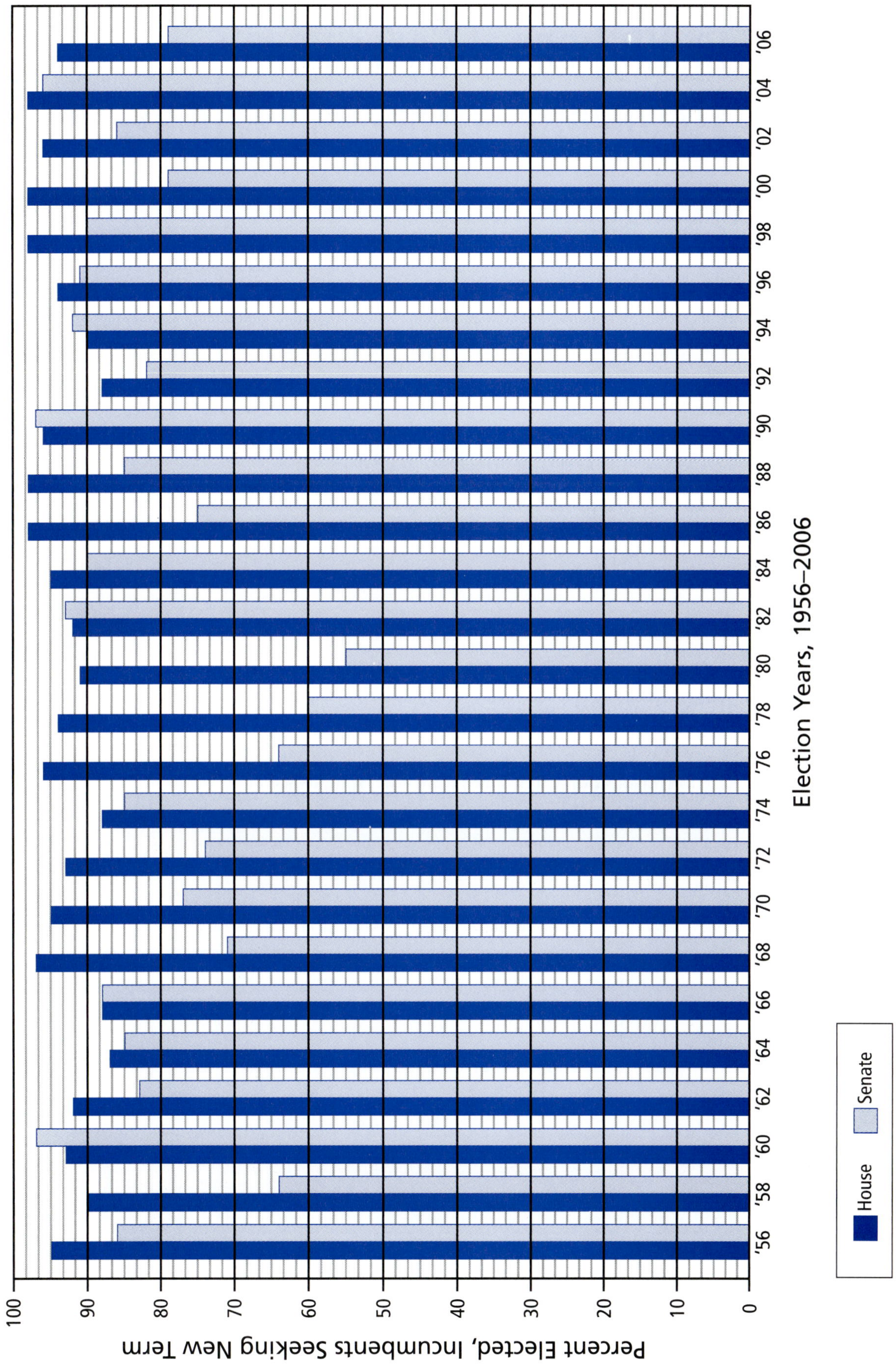

EXERCISE 13

Institutions of Government: Presidential Vetoes and Veto Overrides

Background

Review the requirements for Congress to override a President's veto.

Interpret the Data

Study the table, then answer the following questions.

1. What conclusions can you draw from the data about the level of difficulty in overriding a President's veto?
2. Based on the historical data, about what percent of the time does Congress override a Presidential veto?
3. What factors may explain this?

PRESIDENTIAL VETOES AND VETO OVERRIDES

President	Congresses	Total Vetoes	Veto Overrides
George Washington	1–4	2	0
John Adams	5–6	0	0
Thomas Jefferson	7–10	0	0
James Madison	11–14	7	0
James Monroe	15–18	1	0
John Quincy Adams	19–20	0	0
Andrew Jackson	21–24	12	0
Martin Van Buren	25–26	1	0
William H. Harrison	27	0	0
John Tyler	27–28	10	1
James Polk	29–30	3	0
Zachary Taylor	31	0	0

President	Congresses	Total Vetoes	Veto Overrides
Millard Fillmore	31–32	0	0
Franklin Pierce	33–34	9	5
James Buchanan	35–36	7	0
Abraham Lincoln	37–39	7	0
Andrew Johnson	39–40	29	15
Ulysses S. Grant	41–44	93	4
Rutherford B. Hayes	45–46	13	1
James Garfield	47	0	0
Chester A. Arthur	47–48	12	1
Grover Cleveland	49–50	414	2
Benjamin Harrison	51–52	44	1
Grover Cleveland	53–54	170	5
William McKinley	55–57	42	0
Theodore Roosevelt	57–60	82	1
William H. Taft	61–62	39	1
Woodrow Wilson	63–66	44	6
Warren G. Harding	67	6	0
Calvin Coolidge	68–70	50	4
Herbert Hoover	71–72	37	3
Franklin D. Roosevelt	73–79	635	9
Harry Truman	79–82	250	12
Dwight Eisenhower	83–86	181	2
John F. Kennedy	87–88	21	0
Lyndon B. Johnson	88 –90	30	0
Richard M. Nixon	91–93	43	7
Gerald R. Ford	93–94	66	12
James Earl Carter	95–96	31	2
Ronald Reagan	97–100	78	9
George H. W. Bush	101–102	44	1
William J. Clinton	103–106	37	2
George W. Bush	107–110	4	0
Total		**2,554**	**106**

EXERCISE 14

Institutions of Government: Confirmation of Judicial Nominations

Background

Review the process by which new judges are appointed to positions in the district and circuit courts of the federal judicial system. Focus on the respective roles of the President and the U.S. Senate in this process.

Interpret the Data

Answer the following questions:

1. What are the steps involved in appointing a federal judge? Describe the roles and responsibilities of the participants in this process.
2. Define the terms ***unified government*** and ***divided government***.

Study Table 1 and Table 2 carefully. Then answer the following:

3. Overall, about how frequently does the Senate confirm the judicial nominees sent by Presidents?
4. How frequently does the Senate confirm the judicial nominees sent by the President in a unified government?
5. What reasons might explain your answer to the previous question?
6. How frequently does the Senate confirm the judicial nominees sent by the President in a divided government?
7. What reasons might explain your answer to the previous question?

Table 1 — Confirmation of Judicial Nominations

Years	President, Party	Congress	Nominations Confirmed, %	Nominations to Senate	Confirmed by Senate
1977–78	James Earl Carter, D	95th	92.8%	69	64
1979–80		96th	90.4%	219	198
1981–82	Ronald Reagan, R	97th	96.7%	91	88
1983–84		98th	74.3%	101	75
1985–86		99th	90.8%	141	128
1987–88		100th	79.2%	106	84
1989–90	George H. W. Bush, R	101st	93.3%	75	70
1991–92		102nd	68.0%	178	121
1993–94	William J. Clinton, D	103rd	90.1%	141	127
1995–96		104th	69.5%	105	73
1997–98		105th	80.0%	125	100
1999–2000		106th	61.5%	117	72

D = Democrat
R = Republican

Table 2 — Party Division in the U.S. Senate

95th–106th Congresses				
Years	Congress	Democrats	Republicans	Independents
1977–78	95th	61	38	1
1979–80	96th	58	41	1
1981–82	97th	46	53	1
1983–84	98th	46	54	0
1985–86	99th	47	53	0
1987–88	100th	55	45	0
1989–90	101st	55	45	0
1991–92	102nd	56	44	0
1993–94	103rd	57	43	0
1995–96	104th	48	52	0
1997–98	105th	45	55	0
1999–2000	106th	45	55	0

EXERCISE 15

Public Policy: The Federal Budget

Background

Be able to define and discuss the following terms:

- Revenues
- Outlays
- Mandatory spending
- Discretionary spending
- Debt
- Surplus
- Deficit
- Compound Interest

Interpret the Data

Study Table 1 and Table 2 carefully. Then study the pie charts in Figures 1–8 following Table 2. The pie charts are a good way to visualize the data in the table.
Answer the following:

1. List the years in which the federal government has had a budget surplus and the amount.
2. List the years in which the federal government has had a budget deficit and the amount.
3. Identify a trend or pattern in the federal debt during the years 2000–2007. Discuss why this may have occurred.
4. Identify a trend or pattern in the percentage of spending on interest on the national debt during the years 2000–2007. Discuss why this may have occurred.
5. Identify a trend in mandatory spending during the years 2000–2007. Discuss reasons for this trend.
6. Identify a trend in discretionary spending during the years 2000–2007. Discuss reasons for this trend.
7. What is likely to happen to the national debt if these trends continue?

Table 1 — U.S. Federal Revenues, Outlays, Deficits/Surpluses, and Public Debt 2000 to 2007, in Billions of Dollars

Year	Revenues	Outlays	Deficit (–) / Surplus	Debt Held by Public
2000	2,026	1,789	236	3,410
2001	1,991	1,863	128	3,320
2002	1,853	2,011	–158	3,540
2003	1,783	2,160	–378	3,913
2004	1,880	2,293	–413	4,296
2005	2,154	2,472	–318	4,592
2006	2,407	2,655	–248	4,829
2007	2,568	2,729	–161	5,035

Table 2 — Major Federal Spending Categories 2000 to 2007, in Billions of Dollars

Year	Total Outlays	Mandatory Spending	Discretionary Spending	Net Interest
2000	1,789	951	615	223
2001	1,863	1,008	649	206
2002	2,011	1,106	734	171
2003	2,160	1,182	825	153
2004	2,293	1,237	896	160
2005	2,472	1,320	969	184
2006	2,655	1,412	1,017	227
2007	2,729	1,451	1,041	237

Figure 1 — Major Federal Spending Categories, 2000

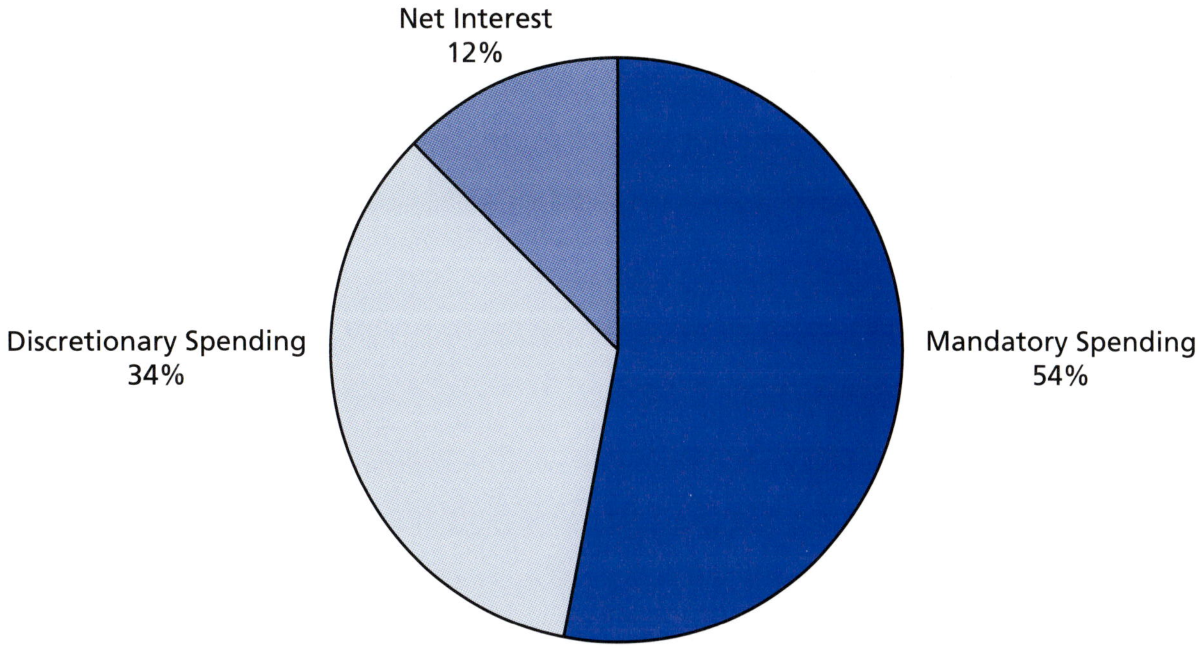

Figure 2 — Major Federal Spending Categories, 2001

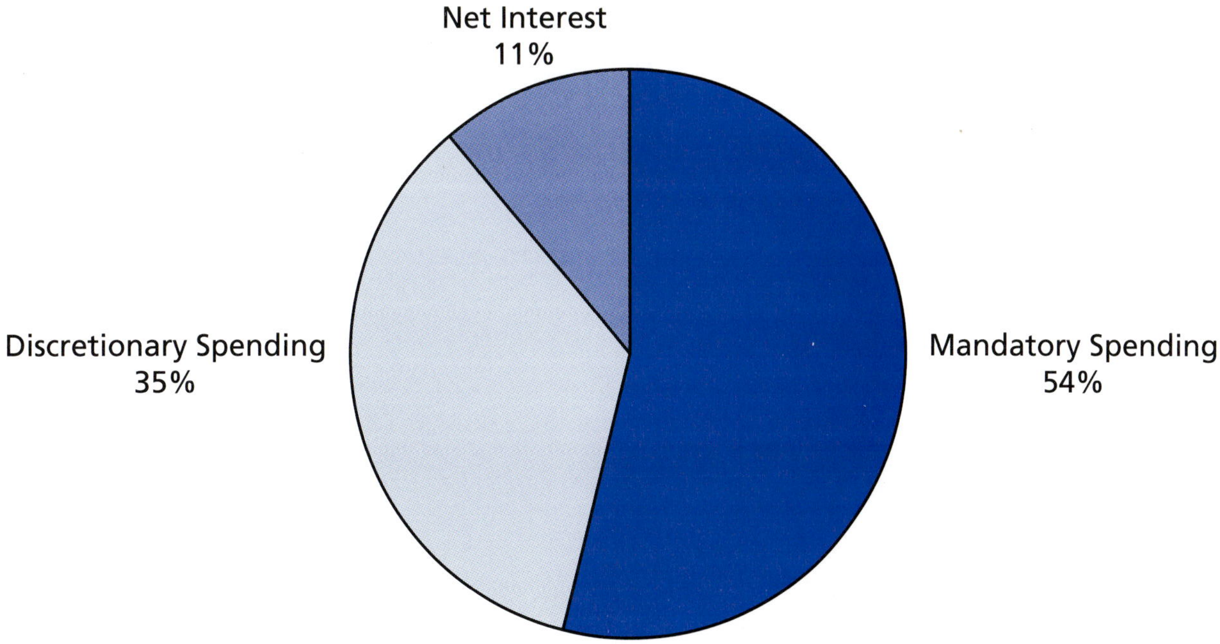

Figure 3 — Major Federal Spending Categories, 2002

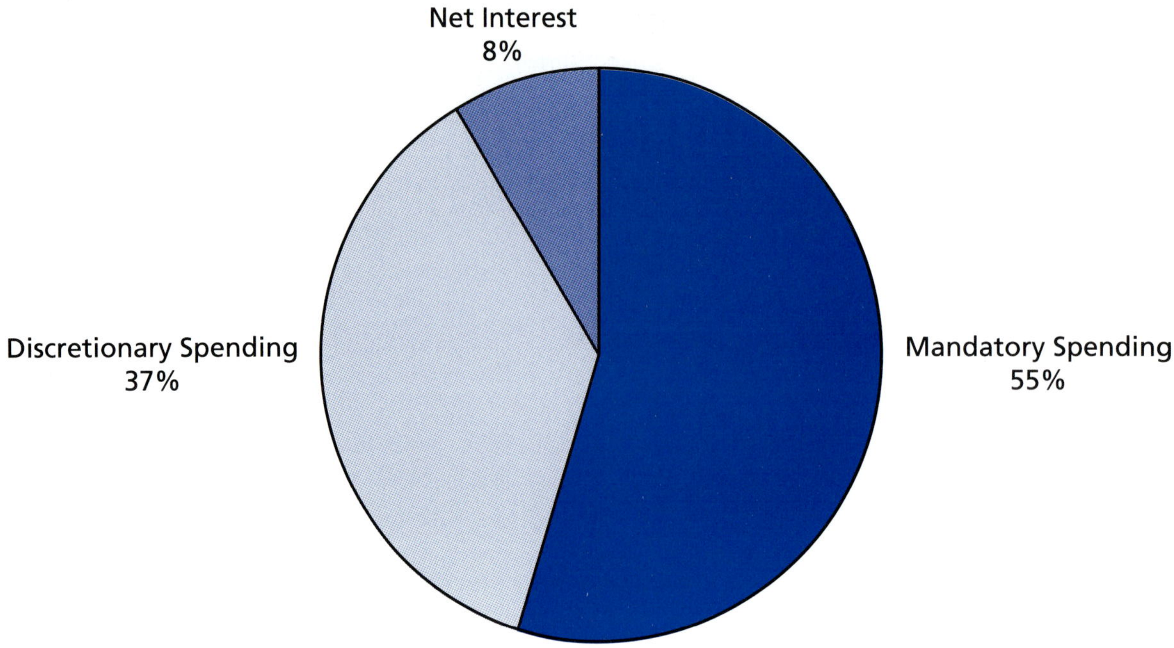

Figure 4 — Major Federal Spending Categories, 2003

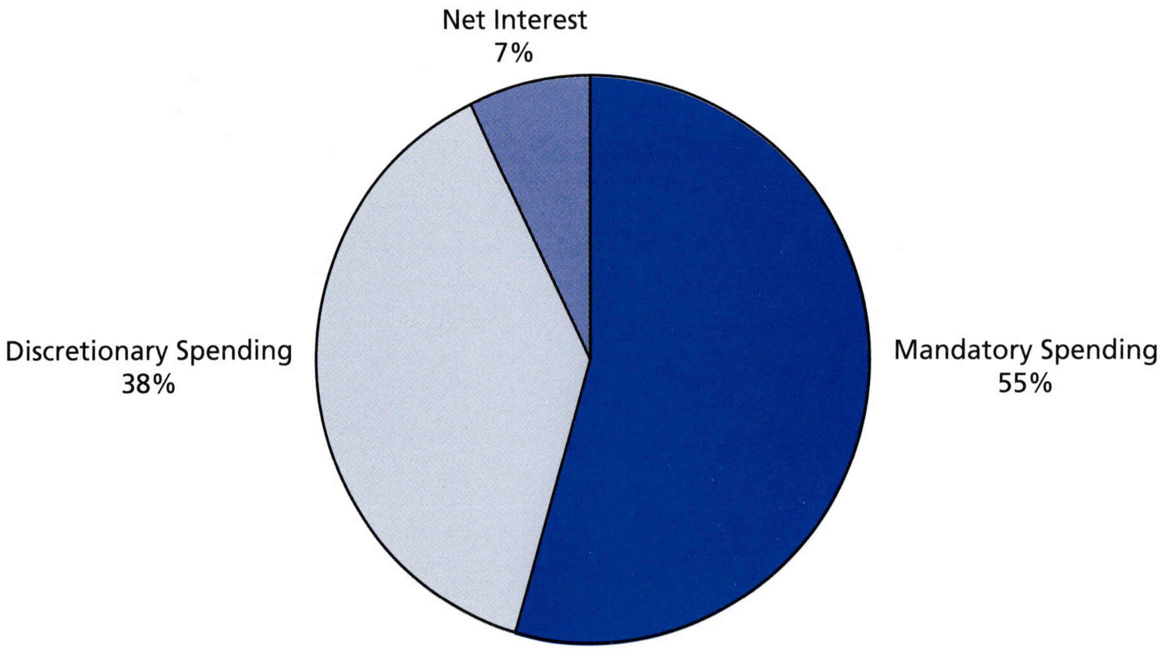

Figure 5 — Major Federal Spending Categories, 2004

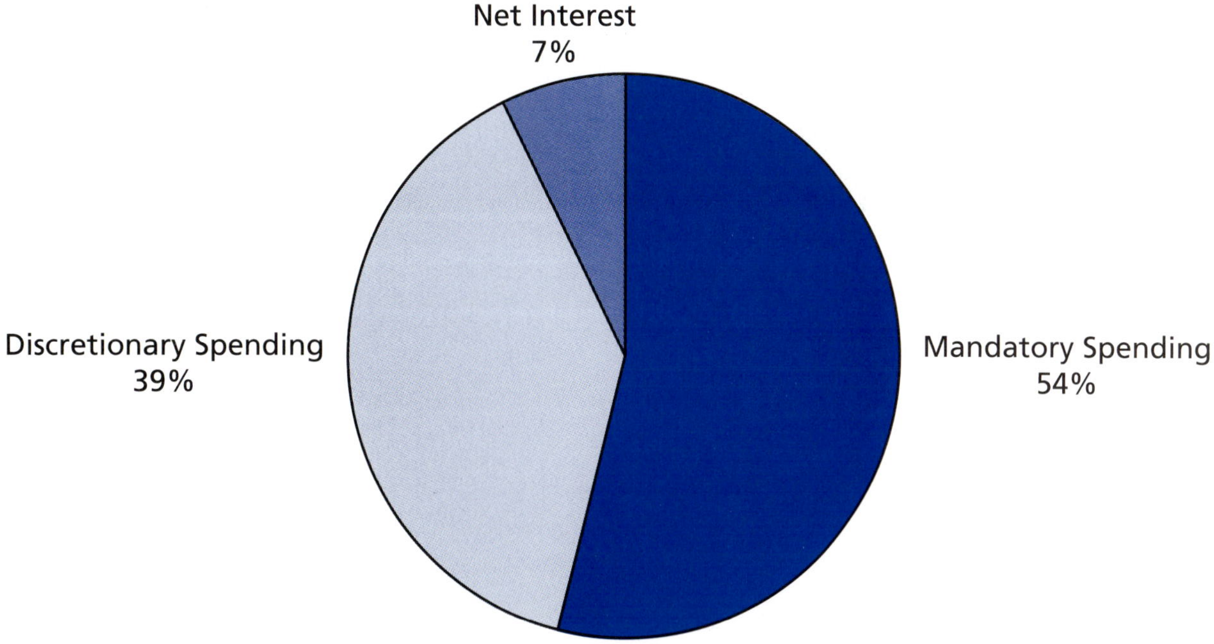

Figure 6 — Major Federal Spending Categories, 2005

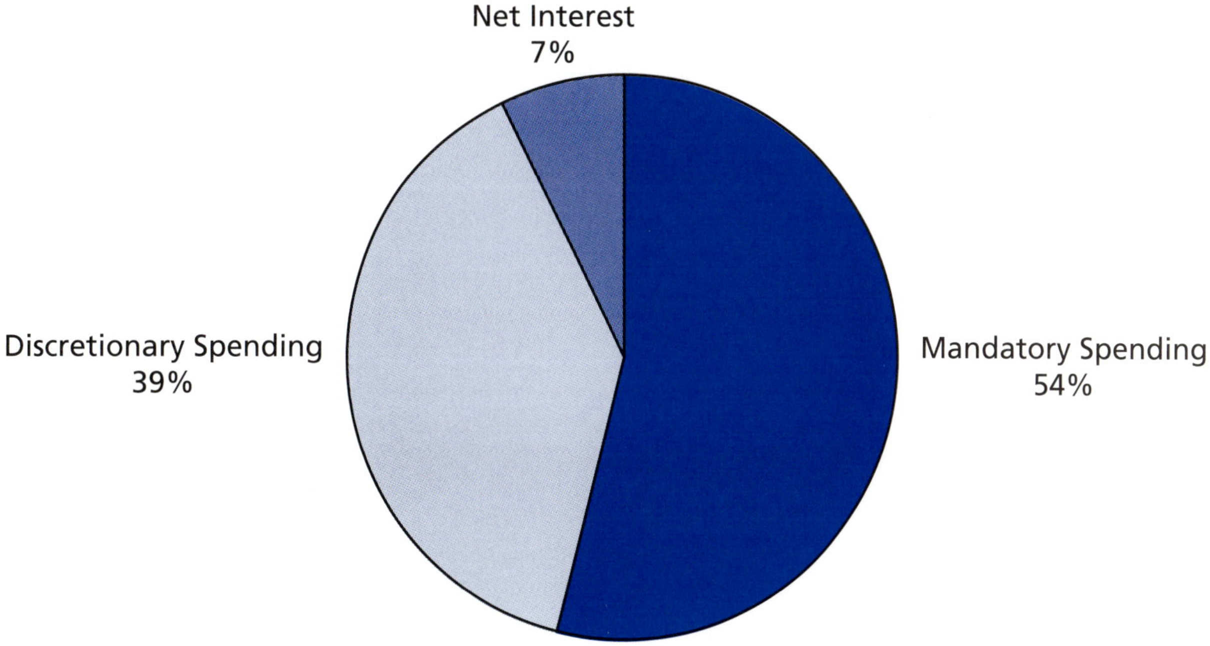

Figure 7 — Major Federal Spending Categories, 2006

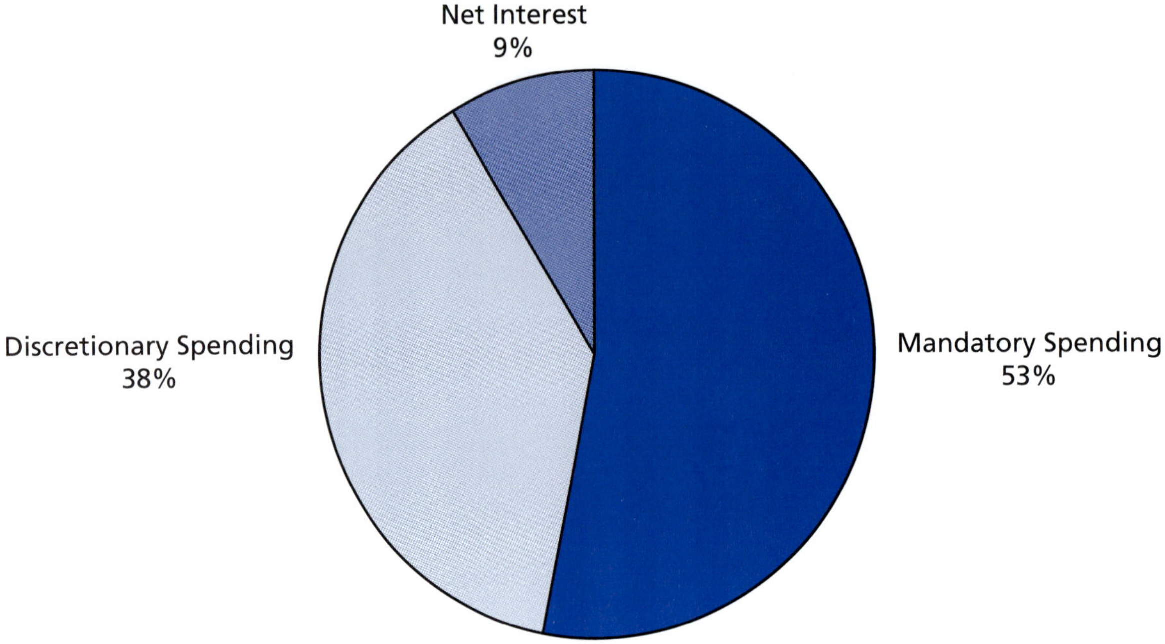

Figure 8 — Major Federal Spending Categories, 2007

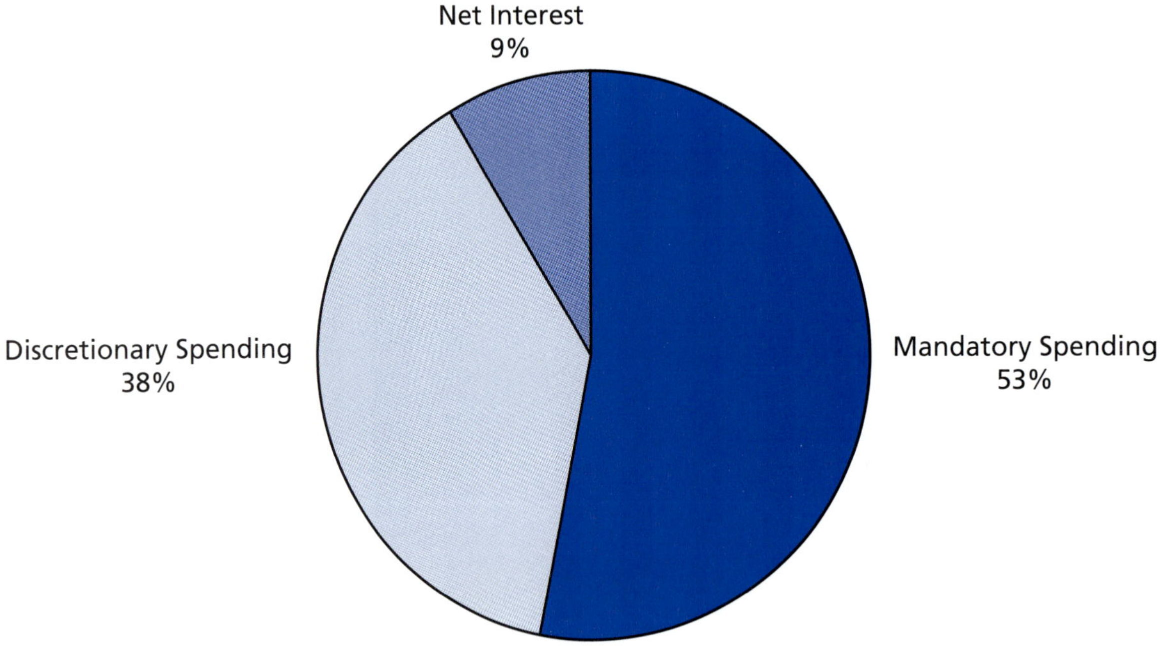

Review Questions

Use Figure 1 to answer question 1.

1. Examine Figure 1. Using your knowledge of government and the information in the graph, which of the following is the best explanation for the trend?
   a) The state governments are gaining more power over the federal government.
   b) It is more popular for citizens to work at the state level than it is to work at the federal level.
   c) The state governments have had to hire more employees due to mandates by the federal government.
   d) The Supreme Court has required that states increase their hiring.
   e) The federal government cannot raise sufficient funds to hire as many employees as the state government.

Figure 1 — Public Employees: Comparison of Federal and State Employment

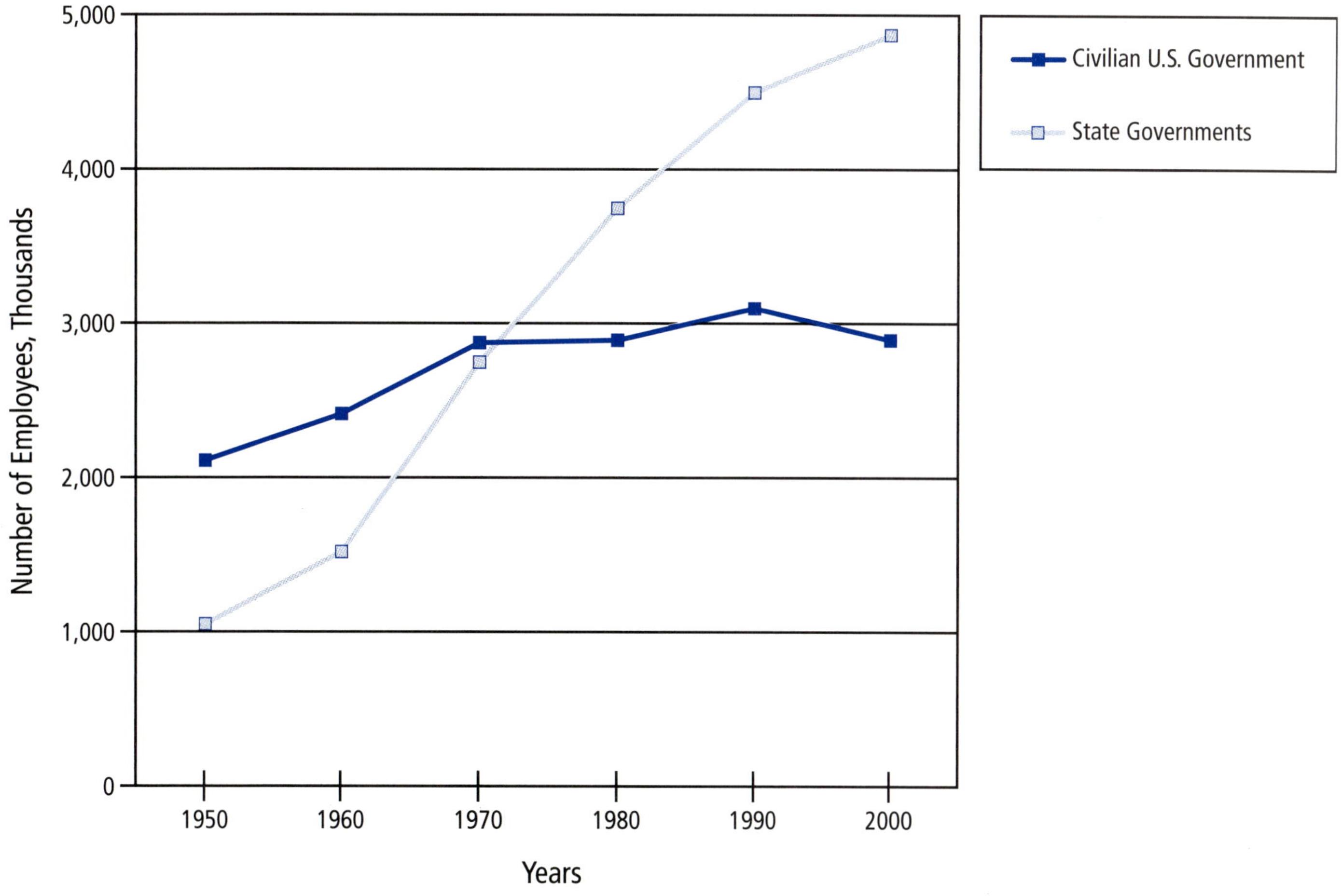

Use Figure 2 to answer question 2.

2. Examine Figure 2. Which of the following choices best explains the pattern of voter turnout shown in the graph?

a) The low level of efficacy in the United States

b) Decreasing levels of trust and confidence in government

c) The realignment movement

d) The decline in the number of citizens eligible to vote

e) Renewal in the importance of state and local government

Figure 2 — Voting-Age Population: Percent Who Registered / Percent Who Voted

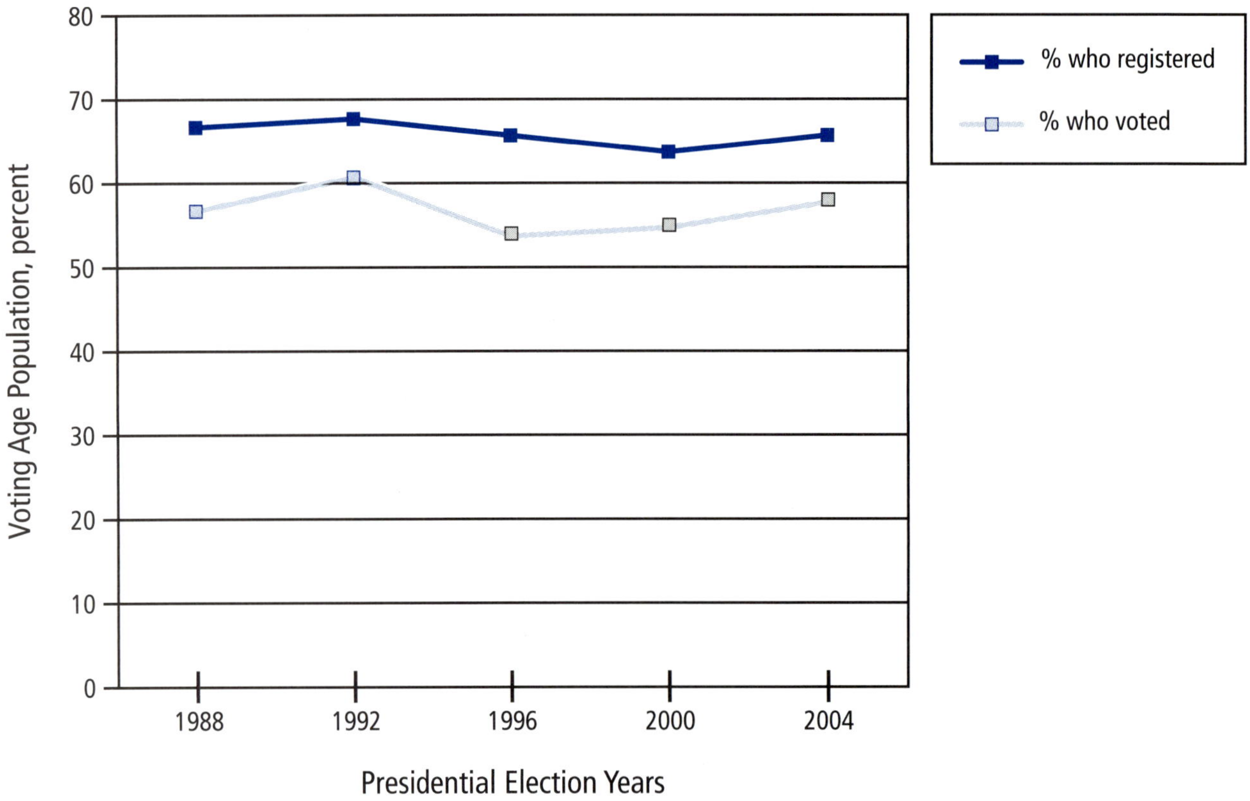

Use Table 1 to answer questions 3 and 4.

TABLE 1

	% of All Votes Received
Candidate A	49
Candidate B	26
Candidate C	25

3. Assume the election results shown in Table 1 are to determine the number of 200 delegates being sent to the Democratic national convention. Which of the statements below is correct?

a) Candidate A will receive 200 delegates, and Candidates B and C will receive 0 delegate votes.

b) Candidate A will receive 98 delegates, Candidate B will receive 52 delegates, and Candidate C will receive 50 delegate votes.

c) A runoff election will be held between Candidate A and Candidate B.

d) Candidate A will receive 49 delegates, Candidate B will receive 26 delegates, and Candidate C will receive 25 delegates.

e) A runoff election will be held between Candidates B and C.

4. All of the following are true about the election above EXCEPT

a) If the election above were held using a winner take all rule, Candidate A would win all of the results.

b) if the election above were held using a plurality rule the winner would have a difficult time claiming a mandate to govern.

c) Candidate C has the most to gain if the system used is proportional representation.

d) A runoff may be held between Candidate A and Candidate B.

e) No matter what rules are used, Candidate A is the winner of the election.

Use Figure 3 to answer question 5.

5. The trend in the number of Political Action Committees over the years shown in the graph is most likely due to

a) an increase in the population

b) a change in the laws regulating PACs

c) new issues being formed with national significance

d) greater freedom of assembly rights

e) a surge in salient issues

Figure 3 — Number of Political Action Committees, 1974 to 2008

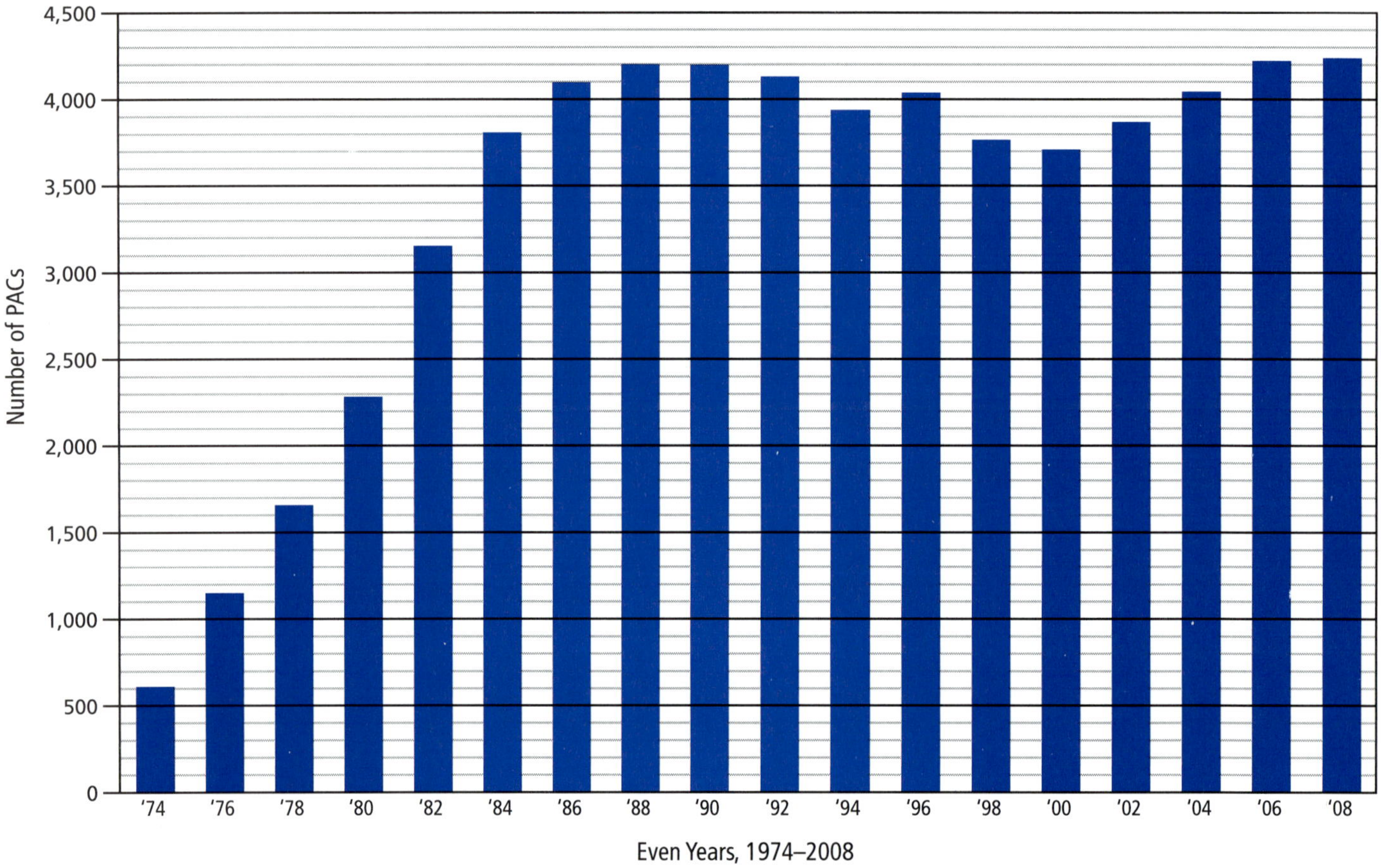

Use the following information to answer question 6.

President's party – Democratic Party

House Breakdown Prior to the General Election: 230 Democrats / 205 Republicans

House Breakdown After the General Election: 210 Democrats / 225 Republicans

6. The election results above are most common in which type of election?

a) Presidential election years

b) Mid-term election years

c) Primary elections

d) Electoral college

e) State elections

Use the table in Exercise 13 on pages 36–37 to answer the following question.

7. Based on information in the table Vetoes and Veto Overrides, which of the following is usually true?

a) Presidents tend to lack power over Congress.

b) There is a stormy relationship between the President and Congress.

c) The President can issue numerous executive orders.

d) The President can wield significant influence in Congress.

e) Presidents are inactive legislators.

Use the data in Exercise 15 on pages 42–46 to answer the following question.

8. The budget data show all of the following trends EXCEPT

a) Mandatory spending is increasing every year.

b) Discretionary spending is increasing every year.

c) Spending on interest on the debt is increasing every year.

d) The total dollar amount being spent annually is increasing.

e) Total dollar amount for annual revenues is increasing.

NOTES

NOTES

NOTES

NOTES

NOTES

NOTES

NOTES

NOTES

NOTES